W9-BCQ-544

THE CHRISTMAS BOOK

Text	**Heidi Tyline King**
Recipes	**Lou Seibert Pappas**
Photography	**Ellen Silverman**
Additional Photography	**Hallmark Cards**
Styling	**Lauren Hunter**

W/O

HALLMARK

Art Director **Kevin Swanson**
Editor **Jeff Morgan**
Lettering Designer **Megan Walsh**

WELDON OWEN

CEO and President **Terry Newell**
Vice President, Sales and New Business Development **Amy Kaneko**
Vice President, Publisher **Roger Shaw**
Creative Directors **Emma Boys and Kelly Booth**
Senior Designer **Meghan Hildebrand**
Illustrations **Salli Swindell**

Associate Publisher **Amy Marr**
Executive Editor **Elizabeth Dougherty**
Project Editor **Maria Behan**

Production Director **Chris Hemesath**
Production Manager **Michelle Duggan**
Color Manager **Teri Bell**

Published by Gift Books from Hallmark, a division of
Hallmark Cards, Incorporated, Kansas City, MO 64141.
Visit us at www.hallmark.com.

Produced by Weldon Owen Inc., 415 Jackson Street,
San Francisco, CA 94111.
Visit us at www.weldonowen.com.

Copyright © 2006 Weldon Owen Inc. and Hallmark Licensing, Inc.

All rights reserved. No part of this publication may be reproduced
or transmitted in any form by any means, electronic or mechanical,
including photocopying (except where indicated), recording, or any
other information storage and retrieval system, without the written
permission of the publishers.

Separated in Canada by Embassy Graphics
Printed and bound in China by Leo Paper
First printed in hardcover in 2006
10 9 8 7 6 5 4 3 2 1
2011 2012 2013 2014

ISBN 978-1-61628-149-6

happy holidays

CONTENTS

Decking the Halls • 10
Decorate your home for Christmas with innovative ideas for tree trimming, homemade ornaments, garlands, wreaths, lights, card displays, and stockings.

Giving from the Heart • 44
Send your love with gifts from your kitchen, personalized presents, imaginative gift wrap, and cards that are dressed up to double as presents.

Getting Together • 68
Gather your friends and family for a sociable tree trimming, a fun-filled cookie exchange, or a casual yet elegant holiday cocktail party.

Celebrating Christmas • 104
Enjoy Christmas Eve and Christmas Day with loved ones, and delight everyone—including yourself—with creative, easy-to-make seasonal menus.

Keeping Memories • 140
Hold on to treasured Christmas memories for years to come with photo displays, keepsakes, scrapbooks, and clever ways to make the most of favorite cards.

WELCOME

All through the holiday season, our homes are at the heart of what means the most to us. When you think back to your favorite Christmases, chances are you remember not only the tree, the twinkling lights, and the presents but also the laughter, love, and companionship you shared with friends and family.

The Christmas Book gives you ideas to make this season of togetherness and warm wishes as enjoyable as it can be for you and those important to you—ideas to make Christmases in your home as memorable, fun, and festive as the favorites you recall. We've filled the book with a wide range of suggestions for activities, crafts, decorating, cooking, and entertaining, but please don't feel like you have to use them all. You can always save some ideas for next year, or the years after that.

To kindle your fond memories, we've included a few personal Christmas reminiscences from Hallmark writers. So thumb through these pages, enjoy their inspiration, and choose the ideas that appeal to you. And, above all, have a very merry Christmas!

Decking the Halls

Decorations bring the beauty and wonder of Christmas into
your home. So whether you're hanging lights, trimming the tree,
setting up for a party, or just getting into a festive frame of mind,
feel free to indulge yourself. It's one of the season's pleasures.

A TWO-TREE CHRISTMAS

My family always got our Christmas tree from the local greenhouse. But one year, we decided to do something different: drive to a tree farm an hour away and cut our own. It was a sunny December day, and it was fun walking the rows and rows of live trees to find *the one*. Finally, we did. Sturdy, full, about seven feet tall—it seemed perfect. The farmer helped Dad cut it down and tie it onto the top of our car.

Back home, my parents set to work putting it in the stand. Unfortunately, that nice, fresh, seemingly perfect tree had a crooked trunk and simply would not fit. Dad cut off more and more trunk until, in his frustration, he actually sawed the tree in half. He was cursing. Mom was about to cry. I was worried we'd have to spend Christmas treeless.

Then a little boy from the neighborhood walked into our garage and exclaimed, "What did you do to your twee?" That got us all laughing. We ended up with two trees that year: the top half of the farm tree on a table in the family room and a nice, straight greenhouse tree in the living room.

Keely Chace

COUNTDOWN TO CHRISTMAS

The days before Christmas fly by if you're focused on all you've got to do. But they crawl if you're a kid—or grown-up—eager for the main event. Either way, a countdown makes each day special.

Holiday anticipation: it's a feeling that you never outgrow. This December, as you count down the days to Christmas, make each one count by celebrating a daily preholiday activity.

As the days of December rush headlong toward Christmas, it's a good idea to slow down and savor the moment, so that the people and things most important to you don't get lost in the holiday hoopla. One easy way to do this is to open your datebook or a notebook each day to jot down something that made you glad or grateful—feelings that reflect the true meaning of Christmas.

To ease the wait for Santa, fill numbered containers—one for each December day leading up to Christmas—with surprises. The twenty-four containers can be whatever strikes your fancy: mismatched socks hanging from the mantel, take-out boxes lined up in the kitchen, or baskets strung along a banister. Tuck a small gift for every person in your household into each container, and open them together at the same time each day. Or play Kris Kringle and leave a simple treat (chocolate, fruit, or even a coupon for breakfast in bed) on everyone's pillow before bed each night.

Twenty-four mismatched socks, each filled with small gifts, dangle invitingly from a clothesline strung along the living room wall.

Countdown Ideas

Arrange twenty-four candles on your dining room table. Light one each night starting on December 1. All the candles will be lit on Christmas Eve.

On December 1, divide twenty-four slips of paper among everyone in your family. Ask them to write a good deed on each of their slips, sign them, and then fold and toss into a jar. Each night, draw a single slip from the jar. The person who wrote the good deed is responsible for its fulfillment.

Want to start counting down later in the month? Create your own version of the twelve days of Christmas with a countdown that starts December 13.

Build holiday excitement by marking the days leading up to Christmas in a new way.

Sweet Treats (far left) Let the countdown begin with twenty-four numbered take-out containers. Fill with candy or other small treats, and mark the progress toward the big day.

Goody Baskets (above) Presents left each night by impish elves help pass the days before Christmas in a happy whirl. Label each night's gift with a glitter-sprinkled number, and place it in a personalized basket.

Sheer Delight (left) Extend the fun of tree trimming by unwrapping and hanging an ornament each night before Christmas. Display the ornaments-in-waiting in numbered bags.

DECORATING YOUR TREE

One wonderful way to feel the magic of the season is to invite family and friends to trim your tree. As you hang special ornaments, you not only connect with one another, you also connect with the past.

The Christmas tree is the center of holiday celebrations. It's where you display the ornaments that make you think of loved ones. It's what you gaze at just before bed to remind yourself that you're in the middle of a very special season. And when the big day finally arrives, it's where you gather to unwrap your gifts.

A Christmas tree offers a backdrop for objects that have special significance to your family. Hanging a crystal bell inscribed with the date of your wedding may spark stories about how you two met or your first Christmas together. Well-loved teddy bears under the tree may bring back memories of your grown kids' childhoods. Your grandmother's hand-stitched quilt makes a sentimental tree skirt. As you decorate the tree and share your tales, capture the stories and storytellers on video to enjoy in the years to come.

Why stop at one tree? Consider personalizing miniature trees for members of your household or decorating them based on themes (see page 22 for a nature-themed tree). Place one in your daughter's room, and hang her swim team medals as ornaments. Hang your kids' clothespin soldiers, pipe cleaner reindeer, and tinfoil stars from the branches of a small tree on your dining table.

There is only one perfect Christmas tree: your own. And it becomes all the more beautiful when it's decorated by the people you love.

Unique Ornaments

Roll small polystyrene holiday shapes (available in craft stores) in glue, then in glitter, and let dry. To hang, knot a piece of satin ribbon into a loop and attach with glue or a straight pin.

To create the look of homemade ornaments when time is short, buy plain metallic balls or fabric ornaments and personalize them with paint pens or fabric markers.

When making ornaments from scratch, use holiday cookie cutters as patterns. Trace shapes on paper, felt, or tin. Cut them out and decorate with yarn, rickrack, ribbon, or other trims.

Ornaments transform your Christmas tree into something festive, sentimental, and truly yours.

Eye Candy (left) For tasty-looking ornaments, fold an 18-inch piece of red-and-white striped ribbon accordion-style, making eight loops. Thread a needle with strands of red and white embroidery floss; knot at one end. Push the needle through the center of the looped ribbon. Next, slip a bead onto the floss, and push down to gather the ribbon together. Knot at the top of the bead and trim, leaving enough floss to loop and knot for a hanger.

Snow-Kissed (above right) Traditional green glass ornaments sparkle more brightly when they're nestled among bright white snowflakes.

Star-Bright (right) Folded-paper ornaments can range from simple to complex ones like this origami star. You can buy origami decorations, or if you're feeling artistic, you can find instructions for this ancient Japanese art online or at a library.

Showcase your personal style by displaying miniature themed trees around your home. Their size makes it easy to decorate one for each family member—even a pet!

Part of the fun of decorating for the holidays is combining ornaments you have on hand with a few new additions. The striking simplicity of this nature-themed tree comes from mixing traditional red balls with decorations made from nature hike finds or craft supplies. To create a similar look:

● Nestle small round baskets or birds' nests in the branches of a miniature tree, and tuck ornament "eggs" snugly inside them.

● Make ornaments from dried oranges and limes. Circle each fruit with jute or yarn, tie at the top to secure, and knot the ends to form a loop. Affix a tassel at the bottom to finish.

● Add lacy contrast with translucent metallic leaves, available where craft supplies are sold. Attach jute loops to hang the leaves from the branches.

● To complete the effect, drape open-weave ribbon on the branches and surround the base of the tree with pinecones spray-painted gold.

CREATE ORNAMENTS WITH YOUR FAMILY

Trimming the tree offers a great opportunity to spend time together. Gather the family to make unique homemade ornaments.

In the wonderful chaos of Christmas, families often get pulled in all directions. Build in togetherness time by planning an afternoon devoted to crafting ornaments.

For one-of-a-kind decorations, have each member of your crew choose a favorite photo to hang from the tree. Simply mount it on scrapbooking paper stiffened with cardboard, punch holes in the top corners, and thread a contrasting cord through for hanging. Create photo corners with satin ribbon. Or buy small frames and add ribbon loops for hanging. For an aged effect, print digital photos in sepia.

A ribbon garland is a durable alternative to the familiar paper chain—and another opportunity to collaborate on decorations you'll treasure for years to come.

Make a glittering snowflake by stringing beads onto a wire frame from a craft store and adding a ribbon loop for hanging. You might want to make multiples to decorate the tree, garnish gift packages, and dangle in your windows.

Embellish gold balls with translucent metallic leaves. Lightly spray the leaves with adhesive spray, and then press them gently onto the ornaments. Hang the balls on your tree, or group them together on a platter as a table accent.

FRESH GREEN FLOURISHES

In any climate, lush evergreen garlands and wreaths—and some faux snowflakes if you lack the real thing—will lift your spirits and remind your visitors that the Christmas season is in full swing.

A house decked out in greenery feels warm and welcoming. So it's no wonder that when the holidays roll around, our impulse is to surround ourselves with fresh pine, fir, and cedar.

Natural garlands and wreaths make an instant impact, inside or out, on banisters, porch rails, and doors. They're easy to maintain because cool temperatures slow browning. Just mist greenery with water daily to keep it fresh. To vary textures and add interest, poke in magnolia leaves, pinecones, dried branches, holly sprigs, or ivy—a trick that also works well with artificial greenery.

Greenery has an understated elegance. When accented with ribbons, ornaments, and lights, the look becomes more dramatic. In cooler climates, a dusting of snow completes the effect. In warmer places, you might fashion your own snow by sprinkling hand-cut paper snowflakes along the length of a green garland (you can press the snowflakes between laminating sheets from an office supply store to make them more durable and weather resistant). To personalize the evergreen wreath on your door, tie on a ribbon bow with a welcoming message written on it.

Greenery is an ideal backdrop for simple holiday decorations, such as these laminated hand-cut paper snowflakes and white fairy lights.

Wreath Ideas

The front door is the classic choice, but wreaths also look great on walls, windows, pillars, gates, and mailboxes.

Wrap wide red velvet ribbon around a grapevine wreath, tie a large bow at the bottom, and add a loop for hanging.

Update a year-round wreath for the holiday season by adding ornaments, red berries, or festive silk flowers.

To make a fabric wreath, bend a coat hanger into a circle (use the curved end for hanging) and tie narrow 3-inch strips of fabric and ribbon onto it, letting the ends hang loose. Continue until the wire is completely covered.

A symbol of hospitality, a wreath on your front door or gate is an inviting way to welcome guests and display holiday cheer.

Garden Variety (left) A lush and leafy wreath of foliage is accented with red berry sprigs. Hang by fastening the fold of a long piece of woven ribbon on the inside of a door and draping the ends over the top to the outside. And remember, you don't have to stop at the front door: wreaths send a welcoming signal when they're adorning other entrances, too, like garages and guest room doors.

Berry Brilliance (above) Holly berries peek through a dusting of snow, which helps keep the berries fresh. For indoor use, spray them with furniture polish to preserve them and add sheen.

Window Appeal (right) A window becomes instantly festive when you use bright red ribbon to hang a wreath from the top of its frame.

LIGHTING UP YOUR HOLIDAY

Lighting does much more than just illuminate. A house aglow with Christmas lights signals the approach of the holidays and gives the outside world a hint of the merriment going on inside.

The rule "less is more" is especially apt when it comes to Christmas lights. Resist the urge to illuminate every feature of your home, inside and out. Instead, place lighting selectively, creating focal points that draw attention to architectural details, like pillars or windows, or special objects, such as a display of wooden reindeer.

Different lights create different moods. Strings of large colored lights set an upbeat, cheerful tone. Twinkling white lights, understated and classic, hint at the season without overpowering the scene. And the low flicker of candlelight lends a cozy appeal.

The Christmas tree, mantel, and banisters are classic places to display lights, but lighting in unusual locations adds unexpected sparkle. For instance, roll strands of lights into clusters and arrange on your dining room table or inside large glass vases on the mantel. Wrap a string of lights around the arms of a chandelier, and use throughout the season instead of overhead lighting. Or line the underside of a glass tabletop with colored lights and throw a sheer tablecloth over it to create dreamy lighting that's perfect for a Christmas party—or a romantic holiday dinner for two.

Why aim for perfection when stringing lights? A kink here and there adds charm to your display.

Festive Outdoor Lights

Make your own yard decorations in any size by twisting heavy-duty bendable wire into holiday shapes and wrapping them with lights.

Focusing a white or colored spotlight on the wreath on your front door is a terrific way to enhance your home's holiday appeal.

Use lighted, star-shaped tree toppers to adorn the decorative knobs on your porch or the tops of fence posts.

Bring some glow to the great outdoors with creative lighting. Candle or electric, lights warm up a frosty winter night.

Lantern Light (above) A grouping of candles, like these displayed in antique lanterns, seems warm and inviting on a front lawn or porch.

Snow Tree (right) If you're lucky enough to have fresh snow, shape some into a tall cone, wrap webbed lights around it, and top with a tin star.

Pretty Pathways (far right) Simple luminarias, used imaginatively, can create striking effects outside. Circle a tree, a pond, or a water fountain with a ring of flickering lights, or illuminate the path to a shed, a garden gate, or a gazebo.

Create a seasonal glow by arranging candles on the mantel with metallic accents. Coil fairy lights in clear-glass vases to add sparkle. Or use cookie cutters to hold votives.

Decorative candles sometimes seem too pretty to use. But don't hesitate to light your candles to create an elegant, welcoming ambience.

● When using candles, remember, safety is more important than looks. Be sure that open flames are kept safely away from decorations.

● Because they reflect light, glass and metallic objects pair well with lit candles. Drape gold garlands and sprigs of silver berries between votives and pillars lined up along the mantel, and accent with metallic star ornaments.

● Wrap vellum around glass votive holders, and secure with tape and bronze ribbon. Line the wrapped votives along a windowsill, or place them in cookie cutters, like these copper snowflakes.

● Other household objects, such as plates, teacups, and cake stands, can also double as candleholders. Use pebbles, sand, rice, or glass beads to steady the candles, if necessary.

● For visual continuity, use candles that are all the same color. And opt for a single seasonal scent, such as pine, cinnamon, peppermint, or bayberry.

SHOWCASING HOLIDAY CARDS

The cards and photos that arrive each holiday season carry memories along with the good wishes of friends and family. That's the best reason to save and display cards throughout your home.

One of the delights of Christmastime is the steady stream of cards from family and friends. Some are filled with news of moves, new babies, and job promotions. Others simply bring good cheer across the miles—reminders of what matters most this season.

With their high sentimental value, your holiday cards deserve prominent display. And you don't need to limit yourself to this year's arrivals. When you combine new cards with old favorites, you'll create an ever-growing collection that reflects the people and milestones that have shaped your life.

To highlight their importance, display your holiday cards in groups—for instance, putting cards in a similar color family together. Pin them to a colorful swag draped along a stair banister, or attach them to a strand of beads, pom-poms, and snowflake ornaments using metallic rickrack (shown here, right).

Display a few favorites under a glass tabletop, showcasing the covers of some cards and the personal messages written inside others. Or tuck them among the branches of your Christmas tree. You might also cover a small tree with cards and place it in the center of your dining table for an original conversation piece.

Decorate the mantel with cards and ornaments
in a winter palette of white, silver, and blue.

On a tabletop, tucked into a wall display, or hanging from windows or a bookcase—your Christmas cards are perfect holiday decorating accessories.

Ribbon Roundup (left) Weight lengths of double-sided satin ribbon with ornaments, and tack to the top of a window frame to make attractive banners for cards. When a ribbon is full, just hang another one as you add to your collection.

Well-Read Display (above) Hang cards from ribbons held in place by heavy books in a bookcase. To secure, tie a knot in the end of each ribbon before you place it under a book.

Card Mobile (right) Suspend cards from a chandelier by punching a hole at the top of each card and stringing it onto a length of ribbon.

A NEW TAKE ON STOCKINGS

Hang stockings for Santa to fill with candy and surprises, or leave out boots, shoes, or even mittens for a twist on tradition this year.

Good things do come in small packages, especially when the packages poke out from the top of a Christmas stocking. To build excitement, hang stockings early and stick candy canes, holly sprigs, and pine boughs inside to hint at what's to come.

Stockings traditionally hang from the fireplace mantel, but you'll discover a number of other suitable spots around the house. Consider the backs of dining room chairs, stair banisters, the kitchen pot rack, and bedposts. Tack your stockings up, or hang them from weighted stocking hangers, which are available in a variety of shapes, colors, and finishes.

Look for alternatives to traditional stockings. You might use actual socks, a charming way to highlight the different sizes and ages of the members of your family. Mittens are another option. Or invent your own stocking stand-ins. Baskets, canvas bags, buckets, terra-cotta pots, and even upturned winter hats can all be filled with small gifts and candies.

Add an international accent this year by adapting customs from other cultures. In France and Sweden, shoes, instead of stockings, are left by the fireplace, while some Eastern Europeans put out winter boots for Santa to fill with yuletide treats.

Think outside the sock: stockings aren't the only footwear you can use to hold Christmas treats in style.

Personalized Stockings

Use fabric paint and stencils to draw polka dots, stars, holly leaves, and other fun shapes on stockings.

Ask people to sign their names with a dressmaker's pen on the cuffs of their stockings, and then stitch over the letters with contrasting thread.

As an alternative to name labels, choose an object or ornament to represent each family member, and hang it from the stocking's loop.

Wrap your stocking like a present. Tack a piece of wide satin ribbon from the top to the bottom, and another across. Add a bow in the middle.

They're a favorite holiday tradition, but stockings don't have to be traditional.

Tea Time (far left) Cotton tea towels can be quickly stitched into stockings. Make different sizes for different members of your family—including pets. Leave the edges of the cuffs unfinished, and create fringe by pulling threads loose.

Fun Flakes (left) A flurry of snowflakes adds Christmas cheer to red felt stockings. Use precut wooden or foam shapes, or make your own snowflakes out of felt and attach with fabric glue.

Sweet Mittens (above) As an alternative to stockings, mittens can be filled with candy and small presents. Mittens a child has outgrown make charming and sentimental decorations.

Giving from the Heart

What fun it is to give! Seeing someone's face light up—and
knowing it's because of your gift—is one of the best feelings of
the holidays. Generosity is infectious. Spread it throughout the
season by giving wholeheartedly and receiving with gratitude.

GIVING A BIT OF MAGIC

No matter how busy we were, my friend and I always had a Christmas lunch, just the two of us. So, as shopping days were dwindling down, we met at our favorite restaurant. As we were finishing dessert, my friend handed me a small wooden box tied with a bright red bow.

"No presents," I said. "Remember? We promised each other."

"Don't think of it as a present," she said. "Think of it as a little bit of magic." Reluctantly, I opened the box, and inside I found a silver star, a sleigh bell, a crystal snowflake, and a sprig of evergreen.

"The star is for wishing on," said my friend. "And it's to show you that no matter what you're wishing for, I'll be wishing, too. The sleigh bell is to keep the music and the laughter in your life. The snowflake is to remind you that you're unique, an original, a very special person. And the evergreen is just my way of promising you that we'll always be friends."

Years have passed, but I still treasure the star, the bell, the snowflake, the sprig of evergreen . . . and my wonderful, magical friend.

Dean Walley

SPECIAL DELIVERY FOR CARDS

All year long, there are people who go out of their way to make your days brighter. This season, show them how much they mean to you by giving them cards in envelopes personalized just for them.

With a bit of effort and imagination, you can transform a greeting card into something that's more than just a card. It becomes an extra-special gesture when your attention to the envelope reinforces the warm sentiments inside the card. And it's easy and fun to jazz up an envelope: just attach a flat ornament, sketch a holiday scene, or add red and green polka dots with glitter pens.

Cards are perfect for those times when a present might make the recipient feel like he or she has to give you a gift in return. A card is a no-obligation way to show heartfelt appreciation. Don't worry about writing a lengthy note. Simply signing your name with a wish for the season will convey your sentiments.

In addition to being a cheerful way to send season's greetings, a card may include a present, such as money or a gift certificate. If you're giving that kind of special card, treat the envelope like a wrapped package. Tie a pretty ribbon around it, and attach a candy cane, a spray of holly, or a special ornament to the front.

Delivering a card yourself makes the gesture even more personal. When you include your entire family, the outing becomes yet another way to share and enjoy the holidays together.

Treat cards' envelopes like gift packages by decorating with tags, bows, and ornaments.

Craft supplies—beads, stickers, and rubber stamps—combined with gift wrap and ribbon are all you need to create memorable presentations for your cards.

Festive Envelopes (left) Garlands aren't just for dressing up trees. Here, alphabet beads strung on silver cord are wrapped around envelopes and attached with metallic stickers.

Bagged Confetti (above) What to do with all those leftover pieces of gift wrap? Run them through a shredder for instant confetti. Sprinkle the confetti inside a clear bag, slide in a card, then use ribbon to tie a gift tag at the top.

Clever Collage (right) Dress up ordinary card envelopes using a Christmas-tree rubber stamp, a square scrap of gift wrap, and a tiny bow.

THOUGHTFUL GIFT GIVING

Well-chosen gifts make people feel special—special because they've received a present that's perfect for them, and special because they're lucky enough to have someone in their life who knows them so well.

When we care about someone, we want to show it. Giving is a natural outgrowth of that desire, and thoughtful consideration is the key to choosing just the right gift.

Finding the perfect gift, however, can be a challenge, so borrow a trick from Santa and make a list. But this is no ordinary gift list. Writing down the hobbies and interests of the people you're shopping for, whether they're knitting novices, country music fans, or skiing enthusiasts, makes finding great gifts easier, even for hard-to-buy-for people. The fun begins when you hunt for or make gifts that reflect the tastes of the lucky people on your list.

For your friend the baseball fanatic, tuck tickets to a spring game inside a paper container filled with peanuts in their shells. Indulge Grandma's sweet tooth by adding cinnamon to sugar and pouring the mixture into a shaker, so it's ready to sprinkle on her morning toast. Homemade fire starters will encourage your husband to relax as he reads by the fire: wrap string wicks around pinecones, dip in melted paraffin, and let dry on waxed paper. Pile them in a basket or box, and top with long matches and a bow.

Paraffin-dipped pinecone fire starters make a thoughtful, practical, and attractive gift.

for you

Gifts of Appreciation

This idea is for the birds—and bird lovers—on your list. Wrap jute around a pinecone, and knot a loop on top for hanging. Coat with peanut butter, and roll in birdseed. Package in a clear bag with instructions for hanging outside.

A coffee mug packed with candy will please almost anyone. Or match the contents to the recipient. Fill with colorful paper clips for a co-worker, red pencils for a teacher, golf tees for a links buddy, or chocolate-covered coffee beans for a java connoisseur.

Delight an amateur barista by filling salt and pepper shakers with latte toppings, such as nutmeg and cocoa. Label the contents with gift tags attached with elastic cording.

Photo magnets will bring smiles to your gift recipients' faces each time they open the fridge. Glue photos to magnetic sheets (sold at craft and office supply stores), cut them out, and voilà—instant refrigerator art!

Give a candle with a holiday scent, such as pine or cinnamon, in a teacup, flowerpot, or Mason jar. Include a small box of wooden matches.

Add a few drops of essential oil, such as lavender, to unscented liquid soap. Package with a back brush and towel.

Many personalized gifts take time and talent to make, but some of the best can be crafted in the blink of Santa's eye.

Art Smart (left) Transform children's artwork, like these collages made from torn construction paper, into one-of-a-kind place mats by having them laminated at a copy shop or office supply store.

Blank Book (above) If your list includes writers, sketchers, or even dedicated list makers, buy blank notebooks and decorate them with labels, stamps, and photocopied images chosen with the recipient in mind. Include pencils tied with colorful cording.

To thank teachers, neighbors, and colleagues for good deeds done during the year, give them potted plants packaged to leave a lasting impression.

When you thank someone with a plant at Christmas, your gift continues to grow and deliver good wishes into the new year. Poinsettias and evergreens are holiday favorites, but fiery red amaryllis or delicate white narcissi are also stylish seasonal choices. Whether you're giving plants straight from the florist or ones you potted yourself, make the package as attractive as the plant inside.

• To give a miniature Christmas tree (left), select a small spruce, pine, or cypress—or even a rosemary plant. Repot in a ceramic planter (or simply set a plastic pot inside), and cover the soil with moss. Wrap paper around the base and tie with raffia. Attach a small star ornament to a wooden stick (a chopstick or bamboo stake works perfectly), and insert the stick into the soil.

• Oversized and infused with color, amaryllis (right) is prized for its brilliance. Place in a terra-cotta pot. Wrap decorative paper around the planter and stitch closed with metallic cording, knotting the end through a gift tag. Secure the paper in place with raffia and finish with a bow of open-weave ribbon.

• Gold gift bags and tissue paper secured with metallic ribbon are time-saving alternatives when you're packaging plants as gifts.

Spiced Candied Nuts

A sweet caramelized coating makes these nuts delicious for snacking or for dressing up a salad or dessert.

2 tablespoons honey

2 tablespoons light brown sugar

2 tablespoons water

1 teaspoon ground cinnamon

2 cups raw almonds, pecan halves, pistachios, or walnut halves

Preheat the oven to 350°F. Line a baking sheet with parchment paper.

In a heavy medium saucepan, combine the honey, sugar, water, and cinnamon; stir to blend. Bring to a boil over medium heat, add the nuts, and boil, shaking the pan, for 2 minutes. Turn out the nuts onto the prepared baking sheet, and spread out in a single layer.

Bake until nuts are a deeper shade of brown, 8–10 minutes. Let cool in the pan on a rack. Use your fingertips to separate the nuts. Store in an airtight container at room temperature for up to 1 week, or refrigerate for up to 4 weeks.

MAKES 2 CUPS

Indulge your family and friends with gifts from your kitchen. These irresistible treats make great impromptu or hostess gifts.

Grace Notes (above) Line the lid of a box with sheet music by cutting it to fit and gluing around the edges, if necessary. If the box lid is clear, cut a piece of music twice the size of the lid and fold in half, so that the music shows through the top. Fill the box with goodies, like dried apricots dipped in white chocolate and candied ginger dipped in bittersweet chocolate.

Sweet Treats (left) Who can resist hot-cocoa mix layered with colorful peppermint candy, chocolate chips, and marshmallows? Packed into a glass candy jar decorated with green satin ribbon and silver bells, the combination is almost too pretty to spoon into a mug.

Cheese Sampler Gift Ideas

For a savory gift, these themed cheese combinations are sure to please. Present the cheeses and their accompaniments on a cutting board, and wrap in burlap.

FLAVORS OF ITALY

Parmigiano-Reggiano

Taleggio

Gorgonzola

Honey, Medjool dates, and salami all pair nicely with these Italian cheeses. Slip in a bottle of Italian wine, such as Pinot Grigio for fans of dry white wine or Chianti for those who prefer red.

INTERNATIONAL MEDLEY

White Cheddar

Manchego

Chèvre

Quince paste (also called *membrillo*), chutney, fresh fruit such as grapes, and a baguette all complement this international trio of cheeses. For wine, choose a Pinot Noir or Cabernet Sauvignon.

DESSERT COURSE

Brie or Camembert

Stilton

Muenster

Crackers, apples, pears, walnuts, and pecans all go well with these after-dinner cheeses. Complement the cheeses' strong flavors with Port, late-harvest Riesling, or Sauternes.

Express your gratitude with culinary classics: wine and cheese, together or separately, dressed up in holiday finery for giving.

Bottle Beauties (above) Wrap wine bottles in sheer fabric or gift wrap, and cinch with ribbons of different textures. Adorn each package with a gift tag or with scrapbooking supplies, such as whimsical tiny metal plaques, hot-glued to a ribbon.

WRAP WITH A PERSONAL TOUCH

A specially wrapped present slipped under the tree is quickly noticed but not quickly forgotten. With stylish yet surprisingly simple trimmings, your gifts will become the standouts of the season.

A wrapped gift symbolizes the anticipation felt in the days leading up to Christmas. Add to the excitement by sprucing up plain wrapped packages and gift bags with quick and easy trimmings.

Browse fashion magazines for inspiration on ways to dress up packages using ribbons as you would accessories. Layer satin bows over gingham sashes, thread satin or velvet ribbon through a belt buckle, or intertwine ribbons of different shades and textures. To add a little shine, tie on a sparkly ornament.

Find a small item related to a package's contents that you can tie to the outside, such as a mini-flashlight or compass to go along with a backpack or pair of hiking boots. Or tuck something special—a teddy bear, a rolled-up beach towel, a colorful umbrella—in a large gift bag so that it just peeks out of the top.

Wrapping gifts can be almost as enjoyable as unwrapping them. A family wrap-a-thon is a great way to boost the fun quotient. Gather the supplies you need, put out the party mix, and crank up the carols. If everyone pitches in, this otherwise time-consuming project just might become a favorite family tradition.

Accessorize gift packages with some fashion flair by adding woven, layered, and belted ribbons.

Simple but unexpected flourishes, such as creative ribbon treatments or a "Special Handling" label, give presents extra pizzazz.

Christmas Contrast (left) Simply playing red off white adds a striking contrast to gift packages. Carry through the color theme with striped ribbon, holiday stickers, and labels. Another way to add impact is to combine patterned paper with patterned ribbon. Subtle patterns in complementary shades make the best pairings.

In the Bag (above) Decorate a plain gift bag with an ornament made from a circle of gift wrap. Use ribbon to add a stripe and a hanger. Or simply attach an ornament with ribbon. Fasten small bags with red and white pipe cleaners woven together.

Tantalizing Textures (right) Bands of colored and crimped paper tied with shiny string add dimension to a wrapped package. Gold cording reflects the sparkle of a metallic-edged ribbon that's nearly as wide as the box it encircles.

Gingerbread Genius (left) For tags almost good enough to eat, trace around a cookie cutter and cut out gingerbread men from speckled card stock. Trim in rickrack and address with a white crayon.

Go Green (below) The beauty of this tag lies in its simplicity. A sprig of greenery cut from your yard or Christmas tree and secured with a bright red bow adds a fresh and natural look.

Nifty Notions (right) Raid your sewing box for buttons, fabric scraps, and felt for crafting tags. Give a reindeer a red pom-pom nose, or sew buttons to make a snowman and outfit him with a ribbon scarf (this satin one has a preprinted greeting).

Homemade or personalized store-bought gift tags add a bit of originality to packages—and they're attractive enough to hang on the Christmas tree once the presents have been opened.

happy holidays

TO Emily

FROM Sophie

Getting Together

Caroling with neighbors. Cocktails with old college friends

and new work colleagues. Christmas morning with family. The

holidays offer dozens of reasons to gather, but nothing trumps

connecting with the people you love—and love to be around.

SPONTANEOUS SONG

On a snowy December 22, my wife and I invited several of our close friends over for an evening of post-shopping eggnog and relaxing conversation before we all scattered to our extended families for the holidays. Someone began noodling at the piano, and the talk turned to caroling. Hadn't it been fun when we were kids? Why didn't anyone do it anymore? On the spur of the moment, we decided to sally forth into our subdivision and serenade our carol-deprived neighbors.

After hastily downloading some lyrics from the Internet and scrounging up several flashlights, off we went into the night—seven adults, three kids, and a golden retriever. At the first few stops, people didn't seem to know what to make of our ragtag band. One house even turned out the lights!

But at the fourth house, the doors opened wide, the family applauded us, and the kids even passed out candy canes. At the next house, the couple asked if they could join us. Others, seeing or hearing us pass by, came out to join us as well. By the time we came to the end of our street, there were nearly thirty of us raising our voices to the sky. Today, what began as a lark has become an annual neighborhood tradition.

Rich Pauli

TREE TRIMMING GET-TOGETHER

Come as you are, come when you can, and come prepared to have a good time—that's the only invitation you'll need to extend to family and friends when inviting them over to trim your tree.

When you host a tree-trimming party, you give family and friends a chance to gather together to share their stories of Christmases past—and perhaps make some memories for the future.

Consider having the party in the afternoon, when there will be fewer parties conflicting with yours and families can bring children without worrying about missed bedtimes.

Make it easy for guests to join in the fun by having the tree in its stand and its decorations unwrapped and set out in baskets or boxes. Ornaments both dress up the tree and spark memories. You might want to share the stories of family favorites as they're hung on the branches: the heirloom bell Grandma brought from her home country or the cardboard reindeer your daughter made with just one antler because she was unicorn crazy that year.

To encourage mingling, serve easy-to-handle finger foods and set out platters in prime gathering spots, like the kitchen. Keep the offerings simple: wine and cider, fruit and vegetables with dip, bakery-bought cookies and brownies, and an array of mini-quiches, popovers, and cheese puffs hot from the oven—compliments of the frozen-foods aisle of your grocery store.

TRIM YOUR TREE WITH NOT-SO-SECRET WISHES

Christmas is a time of hope. Share your dreams—big and small—by jotting them down and creating a tree of wishes.

Chances are you've wished upon a star, but have you tried wishing on a tree? You can make your Christmas tree a tree of wishes by asking friends and family to write down their hopes for the year ahead. Some are sure to be grand, such as "Peace on Earth," while others will be closer to home, along the lines of "Dream Job" or "Cubs Win World Series." Kids' wishes will probably give you ideas for your shopping list or maybe some insight into their secret desires, such as "Baby Sister" or "Chocolate Lab Puppy."

Cut out paper ornaments in whatever colors and shapes you like, such as red cardinals or white snowmen, and add yarn loops for hanging. Set up a table near the tree with the paper ornaments, slips of plain paper, glue sticks, and markers or pens. Invite each guest to write a wish on a slip of paper, glue the paper to an ornament, and hang it on the tree. By the end of the afternoon, your tree will be adorned with wishes, and you'll have lasting reminders of the hopes that this special season brings.

Turn good wishes into good deeds by suggesting guests bring toys to donate to charity. For a guest book, take photos of guests with the toys that they bring. After the party, make delivering the donations a family affair.

Giving guests ornaments tagged with personal messages lets them know how much they mean to you—this year and every year that they hang the ornaments on their trees.

Send your guests home with commemorative ornaments—anything from simple red balls to collectible keepsakes—to remind them of your party and the laughter and memories shared there.

● Write your name and the date of your party or something even simpler, like "Tree Trim 2006," on a card or a gift tag and attach it to each ornament. If you have time, write guests personal messages thanking them for coming and for their friendship.

● You can also transform plain ornaments into take-home souvenirs by writing directly on them with a permanent marker or glitter pen.

● Line up your gift ornaments on a tabletop or along the mantel. Or pile them in a large basket by the door. Whatever spot you choose, they'll make a wonderful addition to your party decor.

HOST A COOKIE EXCHANGE

A cookie exchange might be the sweetest Christmas party of all. Share your family's holiday recipes and taste your friends' favorites at a fun—and practical—swap-and-sample get-together.

Gingersnaps, snickerdoodles, or classic sugar stars? This year, even if you're short on time for holiday baking, you don't have to limit yourself to just one kind of cookie. Invite friends and family to join you in a cookie exchange, and you'll all have several different varieties on hand to nibble throughout the season.

An annual favorite, a cookie swap combines two of the holiday's most-enjoyed activities: visiting with friends and baking. The party itself requires little planning. Send out invitations well in advance, asking guests to bring two or three dozen cookies and copies of the recipe they used. You might also request that they send you their recipes ahead of time by e-mail or post so that you can compile them into a booklet for your guests.

As hostess, you provide some cookies of your own (we offer some recipe ideas on pages 85 and 86), as well as drinks and serving platters. As your guests arrive, ask them to set aside a dozen or so cookies for everyone to munch on during the party and to display the rest in a separate area for swapping. The fun begins when your guests start sampling all the different sweet treats to determine which ones will fill their take-home bags.

SERVE UP COOKIES AND CONVERSATION

A cookie swap lets your guests nibble on a mouthwatering array of sweets. Trade treats and recipes with your favorite bakers.

The cookies at a cookie exchange are as varied as the guests who bring them. Some people use the party as an excuse to test new recipes. Others show off their baking skills by whipping up their prized secret recipes or old family favorites. The variety makes for both an interesting array of tastes and a surefire conversation starter.

Host your party at the beginning of the season. That way, guests can bake their cookies before the holiday rush starts. It also gives everyone a stash of goodies for when sweet treats are needed for an office party, a school function, or a visit from unexpected company.

Part of the fun is seeing who brings which cookies. As guests arrive, have them label their creations using colorful pens and holiday place cards or gift tags. Set out copies of the recipes beside the batches of cookies on display.

Take pictures of the guests proudly displaying their cookies. Use the photos and copies of the recipes to create a scrapbook you can share with guests at future parties.

Consider giving out fun awards, such as Most Ambitious, Most Scrumptious, or Most Liberal Use of Sprinkles, to get everyone involved and to recognize special effort.

HOSTESS MENU OPTIONS

Hot Tea, Coffee, and Milk

Candy Cane Chocolate Drops

Christmas Biscotti

Lemon Tea Wafers

Coconut-Pecan Bars

Sugar Cookies

Add to the festivities by giving your guests personalized containers they can use to carry their cookies home in style. To keep the cookies fresh, slip them into zippered plastic bags before they go into the containers.

If you want to send each guest home with a reusable container, scan a holiday image, print it onto iron-on transfer paper, and fuse it onto a small canvas bag. Other nifty take-home containers are classic cookie tins or red or green plastic buckets lined with tissue paper, with bows tied around the handles. Or use a glitter pen or permanent marker to write each guest's name and the date on a gift bag or around the rim of a decorative holiday paper plate.

Candy Cane Chocolate Drops

Crushed candy canes give these easy-to-make chocolate cookies a refreshing minty taste. If you prefer a subtler flavor and melt-in-your-mouth texture, substitute a cup of white chocolate chips for the candy canes.

Preheat the oven to 350°F. Line 2 baking sheets with parchment paper.

In a medium bowl, microwave the chocolate and butter until melted, and stir until combined. Stir in the sugar, eggs, and vanilla, and mix until blended. In another bowl, stir together the flour and baking powder, and stir into the chocolate mixture. Stir in the nuts and candy canes.

Drop by rounded tablespoons onto the prepared baking sheets, spacing 1½ inches apart. Bake for 12 minutes or just until set. Transfer to racks to cool.

MAKES ABOUT 30 COOKIES

8 ounces semisweet or bittersweet chocolate, chopped

¼ cup unsalted butter

¾ cup firmly packed light brown sugar

2 large eggs

1 teaspoon vanilla extract

¾ cup all-purpose flour

¼ teaspoon baking powder

½ cup toasted chopped pecans or almonds

¾ cup crushed candy canes

Christmas Biscotti

These crispy Italian cookies—with holiday colors—can be baked up to a month in advance and stored in an airtight container at room temperature.

Preheat the oven to 350°F. Line 2 baking sheets with parchment paper.

In a bowl, using an electric mixer or by hand, cream together the butter and sugar until fluffy. Add the eggs and beat until smooth. Mix in the vanilla and orange juice concentrate. In another bowl, stir together the flour, baking powder, salt, and cardamom. Add the flour mixture to the butter mixture, and beat just until blended. Stir in the cherries and nuts.

Divide the dough in half, place on one of the prepared baking sheets, and pat each half into a flat log about 14 inches long and 2½ inches wide, spacing logs at least 2 inches apart. Bake for 25 minutes or until lightly browned. Transfer the logs to a rack. Turn the oven down to 300°F.

Let the logs cool for 6–8 minutes. Place on a cutting board, and, using a serrated knife, cut on a diagonal into slices about ½ inch thick. Place the slices on the baking sheets, and return to the oven for 8–10 minutes to dry and toast lightly. Transfer to racks to cool.

MAKES ABOUT 48 COOKIES

½ cup unsalted butter, at room temperature

¾ cup granulated sugar

2 large eggs

1 teaspoon vanilla extract

2 tablespoons thawed orange juice concentrate

2 cups plus 2 tablespoons all-purpose flour

1½ teaspoons baking powder

¼ teaspoon salt

¼ teaspoon ground cardamom

⅔ cup dried cherries or cranberries

⅔ cup chopped toasted pistachio nuts

Lemon Tea Wafers

1 tablespoon grated lemon zest

1 ¼ cups confectioners' sugar

1 cup cold unsalted butter, cut into pieces

2 large egg yolks

1 tablespoon fresh lemon juice

2 cups all-purpose flour

1 teaspoon baking soda

1 teaspoon cream of tartar

1 teaspoon ground cardamom

At a cookie exchange, these thin, crisp citrus cookies offer a delicate contrast to heartier, richer sweets. Mashing the lemon zest brings out its oils.

Line 2 baking sheets with parchment paper.

In a small bowl, mash the lemon zest with 1 teaspoon of the sugar. In a large bowl, using an electric mixer, mix the butter and remaining sugar until crumbly. Add the egg yolks, lemon juice, and lemon zest mixture, and mix until the dough comes together. In another bowl, stir together the flour, baking soda, cream of tartar, and cardamom. Add to the creamed mixture and blend. Shape into a roll 6–7 inches long. Wrap in plastic wrap. Chill until firm, about 1 hour.

Preheat the oven to 350°F. Slice the roll into rounds a scant ¼ inch thick; place on the prepared baking sheets. Bake for 8–10 minutes or until golden brown. Transfer to racks to cool.

MAKES ABOUT 36 COOKIES

Coconut–Pecan Bars

FOR THE CRUST

¾ cup firmly packed light brown sugar

2 cups all-purpose flour

¾ cup cold unsalted butter, cut into pieces

FOR THE FILLING

5 large eggs

1 ¾ cups firmly packed light brown sugar

2 teaspoons vanilla extract

½ cup all-purpose flour

1 teaspoon baking powder

½ teaspoon salt

1 ½ cups chopped pecans

2 ½ cups shredded sweetened coconut, plus extra for sprinkling

A sprinkle of shredded coconut gives these chewy caramel bars a pretty snow-glazed effect. Chocolate lovers can even skip all the coconut and instead stir ½ pound (1 ⅓ cups) semisweet chocolate chips into the filling.

Preheat the oven to 350°F. Line a 10-by-15-inch baking pan with parchment paper.

Prepare the crust: Using a food processor or electric mixer, combine the sugar and flour, and pulse or mix briefly to blend. Add the butter and pulse or mix just until the mixture resembles cornmeal. Pat into the prepared pan with the palm of your hand. Bake for 12 minutes or until golden brown. Let cool in the pan on a rack for 3–4 minutes.

Prepare the filling: Using an electric mixer, beat the eggs until fluffy; then beat in the sugar and vanilla. In a bowl, stir together the flour, baking powder, and salt, and then add to the egg mixture, mixing well. Stir in the nuts and the 2 ½ cups coconut. Pour over the baked crust and spread evenly. Return to the oven for 25 minutes or until set and lightly browned. Let cool on a rack, sprinkle with additional coconut if desired, and cut into small bars.

MAKES 60 BARS

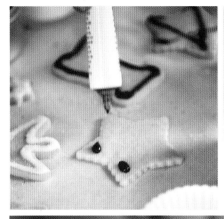
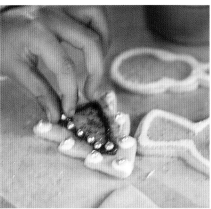

A cookie-decorating station encourages everyone at the party to get in on the fun. Provide plain cookies and decorations and invite kids and adults to make edible art.

A cookie exchange is even more fun when you add a hands-on assembly line so your guests can create their own sweet inspirations. Just let parents know your plans beforehand so they don't dress kids in their Sunday best. And if you have some extra aprons on hand, by all means pass them out!

● To set up the station, clear off a table that you can devote to decorating. Choose a low table for children so they can reach everything easily.

● Before the party, bake plain sugar cookies from scratch or ready-made dough, or buy undecorated cookies from a bakery. Make sure the cookies are large enough for easy decorating.

● Go all out with the decorations. Provide frosting, both spreadable and in squeeze dispensers, in different colors. Put out sugar sprinkles, which you can buy or make by adding drops of food coloring to sugar. Other options include silver balls, candy confetti, string licorice, and crushed hard candies.

A HOLIDAY COCKTAIL PARTY

With good food, good conversation, and good times on the menu, an evening party with your closest friends sets a warm mood for the holidays.

Host a holiday affair that you yourself would like to attend: an intimate and elegant cocktail party that features an appealing mix of food, drink, and—most important of all—your closest friends.

A short, carefully chosen guest list helps keep the event relaxed and unpretentious, and lets you focus on making the night extra special for everyone who attends. Plus, when you surround yourself with only the people you're closest to, the evening becomes that much more fun—a present to yourself during the holiday season.

Another gift to yourself is to keep things simple. Plan a menu that revolves around easy-to-prepare drinks and finger foods. Since you're not offering dinner, you can have your party early or late in the evening, which gives guests a chance to stop by more than one gathering, a plus during this hectic social season.

You know one another well, so there's really no need to plan icebreakers. To encourage some casual snapshots, leave disposable cameras out at party hot spots, like near the Christmas tree, front door, and punch bowl. Later, compile the photos in an album to enjoy throughout the year—and show off at next year's party.

Rather than decorating your whole house, choose focal points in key entertaining areas and dress them lavishly for maximum visual impact.

Decorating for a party gets you in the mood for holiday entertaining. Give yourself plenty of time the week before to get ready, so that on the big day, you can concentrate on preparing the food and drinks and, above all, enjoying the party.

● Light up a room by grouping gilded decorations, such as gourds and berries, across a mantel to catch the sparkle of firelight and give the entire room a heartwarming glow. Combine copper, gold, and silver baubles for a glittery metallic contrast.

● Anchor your mantel display with strong vertical shapes, such as this tall trio (right), and then drape it with long strands of shiny beads.

● The story behind objects can be the unifying element of your display. For instance, Christmas books from your childhood, the angel collection you've acquired over the years, and Nativity figurines handed down by an aunt might come together to create an arrangement that reflects the times and people of Christmases past.

MAKE YOUR PARTY EASY AND ELEGANT

The holidays are the perfect time to indulge friends with an evening of tempting foods, festive drinks, and wonderful company.

Food is a key element of any party, but on this night, easy elegance trumps extravagance. Finger foods, fondue, and drinks that are unusual but easy to prepare make for a menu that is both memorable and doable.

Ease prep time by making appetizers that are simple to assemble, look impressive, and taste great. For instance, cranberry-almond Brie takes ten minutes to put together but will earn compliments all night. The same is true for prosciutto-wrapped dates and smoked salmon cucumber rounds. Guests feel pampered and special when you serve fancy foods—and you'll keep your holiday spirit because making them didn't mean hours in the kitchen.

Toast to health and happiness with flutes of kir royale and glasses of blond punch. One's a cocktail and pleasingly pink, the other's nonalcoholic and elegantly pale, and both look festive and taste delicious. Supplement the bar with sodas and water, and keep a fresh pot of coffee hot.

Dress up each wineglass with a monogrammed tag. Make each tag by rubber-stamping a guest's initials on a gift tag or the front half of a place card. Tie the tag onto the stem of a glass with a pipe cleaner or a holiday ribbon.

MENU

Blond Punch and Kir Royale

Cranberry-Almond Brie

Prosciutto-Wrapped Dates

Smoked Salmon Cucumber Rounds

Bittersweet Chocolate Orange Fondue

White Chocolate Cognac Fondue

The party fare you're serving is as good-looking as it is delicious, so you can keep presentation simple. For instance, a wooden cutting board easily doubles as a cheese board, and white platters create a neutral backdrop for colorful appetizers. Champagne flutes look even more special when filled with rosy, raspberry-topped kir royale.

Two chocolate fondues top off the evening on a richly satisfying note. One is deep brown. The other is creamy white. Both give guests a sweet excuse to mingle while dipping pieces of fresh fruit and brioche.

Blond Punch

Fill a punch bowl with this golden beverage, and add an ice ring to cool it. Or divide the punch between two pitchers, and add ice cubes. For a pretty touch, freeze lemon or blood orange slices in the ice, or float them on top.

In a punch bowl, combine the pineapple juice, lemonade, and ginger ale. Stir to mix. Add the ice. If you haven't frozen the citrus slices into the ice, float them on top. Serve immediately.

MAKES 2½ QUARTS, OR 14–16 SERVINGS

1 can (6 ounces) pineapple juice concentrate, diluted as directed on package

1 can (6 ounces) lemonade concentrate, diluted as directed on package

1 bottle (32 ounces) ginger ale or sparkling water

Ice ring or ice cubes

Thin lemon and/or blood orange slices for garnish

Kir Royale

Fresh raspberries and cassis (black currant) syrup lend a sweet berry flavor and fragrance to sparkling wine. You can substitute frozen raspberries for the fresh raspberries or cassis liqueur for the cassis syrup.

Set out 6 Champagne flutes. (Chill the glasses first, if you wish, by placing in the freezer for 15–30 minutes or filling with ice; discard the ice.) Spoon 1 tablespoon cassis syrup into each glass. Pour in the Champagne or sparking wine, dividing it evenly among the glasses. Float a few raspberries on the top of each drink and serve immediately.

MAKES 6 SERVINGS

6 tablespoons cassis syrup

1 bottle Champagne or sparkling wine

⅓ cup fresh raspberries

Cranberry-Almond Brie

1 one-pound wheel Brie

2 tablespoons curaçao, Cognac or other brandy, or dry sherry

⅓ cup dried cranberries

⅓ cup golden raisins

3 tablespoons chopped toasted almonds

2 Fuji apples, halved, cored, and sliced

2 Anjou pears, halved, cored, and sliced

Dress up a Brie round with dried fruits and nuts, and serve with sliced pears and apples or a basket of thin baguette slices. Be careful not to overheat the cheese, or it will ooze too freely when cut.

Preheat the oven to 350°F. Place the cheese in a baking dish. Prick the top with a fork in a dozen places, and drizzle with ½ tablespoon of the liqueur. In a bowl, toss the 1½ tablespoons remaining liqueur with the cranberries, raisins, and almonds, and scatter over the top of the cheese. Bake for 8–10 minutes or until the cheese warms and softens slightly. Using a wide spatula, transfer the Brie to a cutting board. Arrange the fruit slices alongside and serve.

Prosciutto-Wrapped Dates

½ pound (about 16) dates, pitted

3 ounces mascarpone or Gorgonzola cheese

4 thin slices (about 1½ ounces) prosciutto, cut into 16 pieces

Assemble the dates in advance, and heat at the last minute. Choose creamy mascarpone or zesty Gorgonzola cheese for the stuffing, which complements the salty prosciutto. You can substitute fresh Black Mission figs for the dates.

Preheat the oven to 375°F. Line a baking sheet with parchment paper. Spread each date open, stuff ½ teaspoon of the cheese inside, and wrap with a piece of prosciutto. Place on the prepared baking sheet. Bake for 6–8 minutes or just until warmed through. Serve warm.

Smoked Salmon Cucumber Rounds

1 English cucumber

¼ pound thinly sliced smoked salmon

¾ cup whipped cream cheese

¼ teaspoon dried tarragon

1 teaspoon grated lemon zest

3 tablespoons fresh dill sprigs

Green cucumber rounds draped with rosy smoked salmon make colorful, easy-to-handle appetizers. Ease last-minute preparations by assembling them early in the day, covering, and refrigerating until serving time.

Slice 24 cucumber rounds, each ¼ inch thick (you may have extra). Cut the salmon into 24 strips to fit the cucumber rounds. In a bowl, mix together the cream cheese, tarragon, and lemon zest; spread on the cucumber rounds. Top with a strip of salmon and a sprig of dill.

EACH RECIPE SERVES 8

Bittersweet Chocolate Orange Fondue

A holiday party is a perfect excuse to break out a fondue pot—or two. Serve this orange-flavored satiny chocolate fondue with fresh fruit and cubes of light, slightly sweet brioche, bought at your favorite bakery.

Place the chocolate and half-and-half in a fondue pot over low heat, and stir until the chocolate melts and the mixture is smooth. Stir in the liqueur or vanilla. Keep warm over low heat. Use fondue forks for dipping the fruit and brioche cubes into the warm sauce.

MAKES 8 SERVINGS

1 pound bittersweet chocolate, cut into small pieces

1 cup half-and-half or heavy cream

4 tablespoons triple sec or other orange liqueur, or 2 teaspoons vanilla extract

DIPPERS

Strawberries, fresh pineapple chunks, banana chunks, Anjou or Comice pear cubes, and brioche or angel-food cake cubes

White Chocolate Cognac Fondue

This snowy white fondue provides a striking contrast to its bittersweet counterpart. Brandy or vanilla brightens the flavor of the white chocolate. Rum or amaretto can be substituted for Cognac.

Place the chocolate, half-and-half, and corn syrup in the top of a double boiler; heat over simmering water, stirring constantly, until the chocolate melts and the mixture is smooth. Stir in the Cognac or vanilla. Transfer to a fondue pot, and keep warm over low heat. Use fondue forks for dipping the fruit and brioche cubes into the warm sauce.

MAKES 8 SERVINGS

¾ pound white chocolate, cut into small pieces

½ cup half-and-half

3 tablespoons light corn syrup

3 tablespoons Cognac or other brandy, or 1 ½ teaspoons vanilla extract

DIPPERS

Strawberries, fresh pineapple chunks, banana chunks, and brioche or pound cake cubes

Celebrating Christmas

Christmas comes just once a year, but it can be celebrated in
hundreds of different ways. When the big day arrives at last,
make the most of it by mixing time-honored traditions with
novel ways of sharing the holiday with family and friends.

JUST A MATTER OF TIME

Christmas just can't come soon enough for some kids, and my older brother, Ken, was one of them. One Christmas Eve, after sternly proclaiming that no one was to get up before 6 a.m., Dad and Mom sent us all to bed. Then, after wrapping the gifts, they went to bed as well.

Ken got up at around 2 a.m. and went all through the house resetting clocks—including the one in our parents' bedroom—to 5:45 a.m. He then woke his three younger siblings, and we all ran in noisy excitement to bounce Mom and Dad out of bed. Dad stared at the clock in disbelief.

"Seems like we just went to bed," he yawned, then reluctantly announced that the festivities could begin.

When the last gift was opened and the merriment died down, Ken suffered a slight twinge of conscience and decided to come clean. Dad checked his watch, the only unchanged timepiece in the house, realized what time it really was, and announced with mock solemnity that my brother had earned a spot at the top of Santa's naughty list for next year.

Richard Bagley

CHRISTMAS EVE ANTICIPATION

Eager anticipation is a huge part of the holiday season, and that excitement reaches its merry height on Christmas Eve. Even if you have a few last-minute to-dos, try to keep your focus on fun.

This is the day when checking lists gives way to all-out celebrating. Try to do most of your shopping and cooking ahead of time, so you can devote more of the day to family, friends, and fun.

Keeping the kids busy will help ease their wait. Encourage them to research reindeer online and report back to the family before bedtime. Ask the theatrically inclined to put together a holiday skit and use the afternoon to practice. Be sure to include some physical activity: the secret to sleep on this exciting night!

The celebrating really takes off at sundown. Pop an extra-large batch of popcorn, so you'll have plenty left over for Santa to snack on later. Dress it up with herb butter or drizzles of chocolate and pecans, and then settle in for a film festival. Mix up seasonal classics, such as *Miracle on 34th Street* and *Holiday Inn,* with more contemporary fare, like *Elf* or *A Christmas Story.*

Before the grown-ups retire, grab a mug of hot cocoa or eggnog and sit down in front of the fire to look at photo albums and scrapbooks and reminisce about Christmases gone by.

On the big night, deck your mantel with notes to Santa and ornament-topped glass bottles.

Herb-Butter Popcorn

Savory popcorn is a perfect evening snack, or, if you prefer, try a sweet variation. Make extra for Santa.

6 cups hot popcorn (3 tablespoons of corn kernels, popped)

2 tablespoons unsalted butter

1 tablespoon olive oil

½ teaspoon dried basil

¼ teaspoon dried oregano

3 tablespoons grated Parmesan cheese

Prepare the popcorn on the stove or in a microwave. In a small saucepan, heat the butter, olive oil, basil, and oregano until the butter melts and sizzles; pour over the popcorn. Add the cheese and toss.

Sweet Variations Omit the olive oil, herbs, and cheese. Increase the butter to 3 tablespoons. Heat ¾ teaspoon ground cinnamon and 1 tablespoon sugar with the butter, pour over the popcorn, and toss. Or pour plain melted butter over the popcorn, add ¾ cup toasted pecans, and toss; drizzle with 3 ounces melted semisweet or bittersweet chocolate.

MAKES 6 CUPS

There's no guarantee you'll get everything that's on your list, but you might improve your chances if you leave out some special treats for Santa Claus and his reindeer tonight.

Feeding Visitors (left) Remember to put out some carrots for the reindeer to crunch on. You also might want to set out some munchies, like herb-butter popcorn, to reenergize Santa (and anyone else who happens by).

Hot Cocoa (above) After driving his sleigh around the world, Santa might appreciate a thermos of piping hot cocoa. Ask the kids to help you set it out with a mug, marshmallows, and peppermint sticks.

Filling a stocking can be as much fun as emptying one on Christmas morning. Use your imagination to choose themes and then the perfect gifts.

When stuffing stockings, focus on a special interest of each recipient and look for things that reflect that passion, whether it's art or frogs.

● Fill a budding artist's stocking with pencils, paints, sketchbooks, and any other arty items that catch your eye. A nature lover might enjoy field guides, trail maps, and a magnifying glass. A music enthusiast might appreciate CDs, earphones, and gift certificates for song and ring-tone downloads.

● Tickets to movies, sporting events, cooking classes, and concerts are always popular. Add related extras, like baseball cards or pot holders.

● Tuck in a present that hints at a gift to come. If someone will be getting a necklace, slip in silver polish or a jewelry travel case. Choose the biography of a favorite painter if the artist in your family is getting a new easel or original artwork.

● Buy something for the family, and divide key pieces among the stockings. For example, put a ball from the new croquet set into each stocking, tuck in pieces from this year's in-demand board game, or divvy up computer games for the new computer that's waiting under the tree.

A GREAT START TO CHRISTMAS

At long last, Christmas is here! Wake up to a day of giving, getting, and making merry with family and friends. A little chaos is inevitable, but with some planning, that can be joyful, too.

The sounds of Christmas morning are like those of no other day of the year: the r-r-rip of wrapping paper, the squeals of children playing with brand-new toys, the laughter of people who are enjoying the moment and delighting in one another's company.

There's just one thing on kids' minds this morning: opening gifts. Make sure their stockings are stuffed and within reach to keep the young ones busy first thing in the morning. (With luck, this savvy planning might buy you a few extra minutes in bed.) When the happy chaos of opening presents ensues, maintain some order by having a basket for each person to stash his or her loot. Toss boxes and wrapping paper into a trash bag so you can recycle later, and also so you can check through it for pieces of games and toys that may have been thrown away by mistake.

Once the presents are opened, move the party into the kitchen or dining room for a leisurely sit-down breakfast. While you're enjoying the meal, ask everyone at the table to name a favorite gift or memory from the morning. Have plenty of juice and coffee on hand to encourage lingering afterward.

COOK UP A TASTY CHRISTMAS MORNING

Fuel up everyone for the merry day ahead with a scrumptious breakfast, prepared in advance for a minimum of last-minute fuss.

Make the magic of Christmas last all morning long by enjoying a leisurely sit-down breakfast. This is not a dress-up affair—indeed, pajamas meet the dress code in many households. So come as you are, gather around the table, and take time to enjoy the company.

Simplicity rules the day, starting with table decorations. A red-striped green tablecloth and a vase filled with red berries or festive flowers can be arranged the night before. Slip cloth napkins through napkin rings, such as these miniature grapevine wreaths, and tuck in a sprig of red berries to carry on the theme of the centerpiece.

"Breakfast is ready!" You can say it almost as quickly as you can put a special holiday breakfast on the table. The key is to prepare dishes ahead of time, so that you can pop them out of the fridge and into the oven. French toast and coffee cake can be frozen a few weeks in advance. A frittata baked the day before can be served at room temperature.

One thing to save for Christmas morning is brewing fresh coffee, a necessity for bleary-eyed parents. As a thoughtful touch, warm up the cream in the microwave or on the stove. For a healthy start, serve goblets of fresh orange juice, either home squeezed or store bought.

MENU

Fresh-Squeezed Orange Juice
and Fresh-Brewed Coffee

Sliced Fruit

Christmas Tree French Toast

Cranberry-Walnut Coffee Cake

Artichoke and Sun-Dried Tomato Frittata

Add some holiday cheer to breakfast by cutting grilled French toast into Christmas trees or other holiday shapes with cookie cutters. Serve with a pitcher of warm maple syrup and flavored butter: bring unsalted butter to room temperature and then mix in honey, ground cinnamon and sugar, or mashed berries to taste.

Fruit is always welcome in the morning, so put out plates of some favorites, such as bananas and grapes, and mix in something more exotic, such as kiwifruits. If you're slicing fruits ahead of time, sprinkle apples and pears with lemon juice to prevent browning. And if you received a fruit basket as a present, serve its contents, too.

Cranberry-Walnut Coffee Cake

You can bake this easy-to-make coffee cake ahead of time and store it in an airtight container for up to 2 days or in the freezer for up to 3 weeks.

Preheat the oven to 350°F. Line the bottom of a 9-inch springform pan with parchment paper, and butter and flour the pan sides. You can also use a 9-inch round or square pan.

In a large bowl, using an electric mixer or by hand, beat ½ cup of the butter, ½ cup of the brown sugar, and the granulated sugar until creamy. Beat in the eggs, orange zest, and orange juice concentrate until smooth. In a medium bowl, stir 2 cups of the flour together with the baking powder, baking soda, salt, and cinnamon. Beat the flour mixture and sour cream into the butter mixture until smooth, about 1 minute. Stir in the cranberries.

In another bowl, combine the remaining 1 tablespoon butter, 2 tablespoons brown sugar, and 1 tablespoon flour, and stir in the walnuts. Pour the batter into the prepared pan, and scatter the walnut mixture over the top. Bake 30–40 minutes or until a toothpick inserted in the center comes out clean. Transfer to a wire rack to cool. Serve warm or at room temperature.

MAKES 12 SERVINGS

½ cup plus 1 tablespoon unsalted butter, at room temperature

½ cup plus 2 tablespoons firmly packed light brown sugar

¼ cup granulated sugar

2 large eggs

2 tablespoons each grated orange zest and thawed orange juice concentrate

2 cups plus 1 tablespoon all-purpose flour

1½ teaspoons baking powder

½ teaspoon baking soda

¼ teaspoon salt

1 teaspoon ground cinnamon

¾ cup sour cream

1 cup dried or fresh cranberries

1 cup chopped walnuts

Artichoke and Sun-Dried Tomato Frittata

You can bake this frittata a day in advance, cover tightly, and refrigerate; bring it to room temperature before serving. Canned artichoke hearts (not marinated) can be substituted for frozen. Drain and rinse before using.

Preheat the oven to 350°F. Oil or butter a 9-inch-square baking pan.

In a saucepan, cook the artichoke hearts in salted boiling water 5–6 minutes or until almost tender; drain. In a skillet, heat the oil over medium heat and sauté the onions 2–3 minutes or until soft. In a bowl, beat the eggs just until blended; mix in the sour cream, parsley, and Gruyère cheese. Stir in the artichokes, onions, and tomatoes. Season with salt and pepper.

Pour the egg mixture into the prepared baking pan, and sprinkle with the Romano cheese. Bake for 25 minutes or until set. Serve warm or at room temperature.

MAKES 6 SERVINGS

10 ounces frozen artichoke hearts

2 tablespoons olive oil

6 green onions, chopped

6 large eggs

¼ cup sour cream

3 tablespoons minced fresh flat-leaf parsley

¾ cup (3 ounces) shredded Gruyère or Swiss cheese

6 tablespoons chopped oil-packed sun-dried tomatoes

Salt and black pepper

¼ cup (1 ounce) grated Romano or Parmesan cheese

Turn Christmas Day into an adventure with a treasure hunt where everyone works together to solve a mystery and maybe find a hidden gift.

It may take no time at all to rip through paper and unwrap the presents under your tree. To make the morning's excitement last into the day, stage a treasure hunt for the whole family.

● This around-the-house treasure hunt has toys to construct at each stop. A treasure hunt is also a great way to build up to an extra-special Christmas gift or to hide one that's too big to wrap.

● Put the clues out late on Christmas Eve, or ask antsy kids to create a treasure hunt for their siblings. Drawing maps and devising clues might occupy them for an hour or two.

● Make a map, marking spots where clues can be found. Draw simple sketches (like the ones in the photo, left), or cut images from a magazine. The clues at each spot should point to the treasure, or for younger children, consider leaving parts of the treasure (like the toy pieces attached to the wreath, right) as encouragement to continue.

● To make the clues more challenging for teens and adults, leave out a compass and give directions or write easy-to-solve riddles.

SAVORING CHRISTMAS

Santa has come and gone, but visiting with family and friends has just begun. Mark the occasion by setting a beautiful table, a generous gesture that makes everyone feel welcome and special.

Set a Christmas table that fits your style early enough in the day so that you're not rushed at the last moment. If all the guests won't fit around one table, set up another one nearby. But instead of making it a kids' table, mix up the ages, and play musical chairs at dessert. Or serve a buffet and let guests sit wherever they'd like.

As families grow and branch out, accommodating everyone on such a busy day can be a challenge. So just go with the holiday flow. If the celebration is at your house, pick a time for dinner that works for most of the people on your guest list.

Have platters of appetizers ready for guests who can only drop by before dinner, and have sliced meats, cheeses, breads, and a selection of condiments on hand for stragglers who ate a big meal earlier in the day. Arrange desserts buffet style, so that they're available whenever anyone has the urge to indulge.

Mark the moment with a toast. The words don't have to be flowery: simply tell everyone how much having friends and family gathered together in your home means to you.

Mercury-glass candlesticks paired with clear glass accents bring a soft shimmer to the table. Ivory linens and white flowers keep the look elegant.

Candle Charisma (left) When you want to create instant atmosphere, count on candles. Keep them in the same color family for a coordinated look, but feel free to mix sizes and shapes.

Looking Glass (above) Glass ornaments make great take-home mementos of the day and extend the decorating theme to each place setting.

Flower Power (right) Accent winter white roses with seasonal berries. Low arrangements let guests see one another across the table.

GATHER FOR A MEMORABLE MEAL

There are just two essential ingredients for a wonderful Christmas dinner: good company and good food.

The best get-togethers make everyone feel welcome and relaxed, and Christmas is certainly no exception. Here are some things you can do beforehand to help your guests feel both comfortable and special.

Create an inviting atmosphere that reflects your personality, whether you prefer the formality of china and crystal or enjoy experimenting with different patterns of tableware, linens, and flatware. (If you have a lot of holiday dinner guests, you might need to improvise when it comes to setting the table.) No matter what type of table you opt for, illuminate it beautifully by lining up candlesticks or votive holders in the center and lighting the candles.

Set a small gift on top of each plate. Look for items that coordinate with the table's decor. Here, a glass ornament is attached through a grommet to a napkin ring made from coiled gold paper. Each guest's name is written in silver ink on the paper so it can serve as a place card. For a small group, consider individual presents for each diner, perhaps following a theme that will spark conversation, such as guidebooks for dream vacations. Or add a touch of Merrie Olde England with Christmas crackers that snap open with a bang, spilling out favors such as paper crowns and toys.

MENU

Pinot Noir or Zinfandel and Sparkling Grape Juice

Appetizer Platter

Ham with Red and Green Grape Wreath

Green Beans with Almonds

Mashed Sweet Potatoes
with Browned Butter

Sun-Dried Tomato, Walnut,
and Goat Cheese Salad

Chocolate Soufflé Cake with
Cinnamon Whipped Cream

Plan a menu that's festive but not fussy. Make sure there's something for everybody, including vegetarians and guests with special diets. Ham served with red and green grapes looks stunning. Add browned butter to sweet potatoes and toasted almonds to green beans to make these familiar side dishes extra special. Dress up a simple green salad with tangy goat cheese and colorful sun-dried tomatoes.

Appetizer Platter

While you finish preparing the Christmas meal, it's nice to offer appetizers for snacking. No need to be formal—simply set out platters on the coffee table, in the kitchen, or wherever people gather.

You can assemble an assortment of appetizers from simple ingredients and ready-made food from a deli or the gourmet section of a grocery store. Here are ideas and a shopping list for starters that look special but don't take much time to make. Select a few for your menu.

Bocconcini are bite-sized balls of fresh mozzarella. Skewer each mozzarella ball with a cherry tomato and a basil leaf. Marinated olives are easily prepared at home in advance (see recipe below), or you may purchase a variety from a deli. Toasted almonds (Spanish Marcona almonds are especially tasty), cashews, or pistachio nuts are nice with dried figs or apricots.

Smoked trout is delicious on crackers with a smear of crème fraîche or sour cream mixed with horseradish, and a sprig of dill. You can also add horseradish to yogurt (a lower-fat alternative to sour cream) and offer it as a dip with crudités, such as baby carrots, sugar snap peas, red and gold cherry tomatoes, celery, zucchini, or jicama sticks.

You can serve ready-made hummus on pita bread or on the cut ends of Belgian endive leaves and sprinkle it with minced chives or diced oil-packed sun-dried tomatoes. Prosciutto-draped melon balls or Comice pear slices are also an option.

MAKES 8 SERVINGS

1 pint *bocconcini* (mozzarella balls)

1 pint cherry tomatoes

Fresh basil leaves

1 pint seasoned olives

½ pound toasted nuts

½ pound dried figs or apricots

¼ pound smoked trout

2 kinds of crackers

Fresh dill

1 cup crème fraîche, sour cream, or plain yogurt, flavored with 2 tablespoons prepared horseradish

1 pound raw vegetables

½ pound hummus

Pita bread

2 heads of Belgian endive

Fresh chives or oil-packed sun-dried tomatoes

2 ounces thinly sliced prosciutto

2 cups cantaloupe or honeydew melon balls, or 2 Comice pears

Zesty Olives

Flavor your favorite olives—Kalamata, Niçoise, dry cured—with herbs, citrus zest, and garlic. Toss the olives with the herbs, and let them mellow for at least a week before sampling. These also make great gifts.

In a bowl, toss the olives with the oregano, citrus zest, garlic, rosemary, and olive oil, coating the olives evenly. Pack the olives into 1 or more jars, cap tightly, and refrigerate. For the best flavor, let marinate for at least 1 week before serving. They will keep for up to 3 weeks.

MAKES 2 CUPS

1 pint black or green olives, or a combination

Leaves of 3 oregano sprigs

2 teaspoons grated lemon zest or orange zest

2 cloves garlic, peeled

1 tablespoon chopped fresh rosemary

2 tablespoons olive oil

Ham with Red and Green Grape Wreath

1 fully cooked bone-in half ham, about 8 pounds

⅔ cup apricot jam or seedless blackberry jam

2 tablespoons Dijon mustard

1 tablespoon balsamic vinegar

2 tablespoons unsalted butter

2½ cups red and green seedless grapes

Fresh sage leaves for garnish

Encircle an apricot jam–glazed ham with warm red and green grapes for a festive holiday presentation. Keep in mind that a boneless ham is easy to slice, but a bone-in ham offers better flavor.

Position a rack in the lower third of the oven and preheat to 325°F.

Score the fat on the upper half of the ham in a diamond pattern about ¼ inch deep. Place on a rack in a roasting pan and roast for 1 hour. Mix together the jam, mustard, and vinegar, and spread over the ham. Continue to roast for 1 hour longer or until glazed and shiny.

Transfer to a cutting board, and let the ham rest for at least 15 minutes before carving. Just before serving the ham, melt the butter in a saucepan over low heat, add the grapes, and warm until heated through. Spoon grapes around the ham and garnish with fresh sage.

MAKES 8 SERVINGS

Green Beans with Almonds

½ cup slivered or sliced almonds

2 pounds green beans, ends trimmed

2 tablespoons olive oil

2 teaspoons minced fresh tarragon or ½ teaspoon dried tarragon

Salt and black pepper

To eliminate the step of trimming the stem ends, substitute fresh haricots verts (small, slender French green beans) for regular green beans and reduce the cooking time to about 4 minutes. Or use frozen green beans.

Preheat the oven to 325°F. On a rimmed baking sheet, spread the almonds in a single layer and toast, stirring occasionally, 8–10 minutes or until fragrant and slightly darker in color.

Fill a large pot three-fourths full of water, and bring to a boil. Salt the water, add the green beans, and cook for 5–6 minutes or until tender-crisp. Drain well and transfer to a bowl.

Drizzle the beans with the olive oil, sprinkle with the tarragon, and toss to coat. Season to taste with salt and pepper; toss again. Transfer to a serving bowl, and sprinkle with the almonds.

MAKES 8 SERVINGS

Mashed Sweet Potatoes with Browned Butter

Use yellow- or orange-fleshed sweet potatoes for this dish. You may make it a few hours in advance and then reheat it in a preheated 325°F oven for about 20 minutes. Drizzle with the browned butter just before serving.

Preheat the oven to 400°F.

Prick the sweet potatoes several times with a fork, and place on a baking sheet. Bake for about 1 hour or until tender. Let cool for about 5 minutes or just until they can be handled.

Halve the sweet potatoes, scoop the flesh into a bowl, and mash until smooth. Whip in half of the butter and the ½ cup orange juice, adding more orange juice if a lighter consistency is desired. Season to taste with salt and pepper.

In a small pan, melt the remaining 2 tablespoons butter and heat until it is a light golden brown. Spoon the potatoes into a serving dish, and drizzle with the butter.

MAKES 8 SERVINGS

4 or 5 large sweet potatoes (about 4 pounds)

4 tablespoons unsalted butter, at room temperature

½ cup fresh orange juice, or as needed

Salt and black pepper

Sun-Dried Tomato, Walnut, and Goat Cheese Salad

This flavor-packed salad comes together quickly and adds bright color to the holiday table. You may substitute dried cranberries, fresh pomegranate seeds, or thin Comice pear slices for the sun-dried tomatoes.

In a small bowl, whisk together the mustard and vinegar. Whisk in the olive oil and walnut oil, and season to taste with salt and pepper. In a large bowl, toss together the salad greens and sun-dried tomatoes. Drizzle with the dressing and toss again. Scatter the nuts over the salad, and crumble cheese on top. Serve at once.

MAKES 8 SERVINGS

1 teaspoon Dijon mustard

3 tablespoons balsamic vinegar

3 tablespoons extra-virgin olive oil

2 tablespoons walnut oil

Salt and black pepper

10 cups (about ⅔ pound) mixed salad greens

½ cup chopped oil-packed sun-dried tomatoes

½ cup chopped toasted walnuts or pecans

3 ounces fresh goat cheese

Chocolate Soufflé Cake with Cinnamon Whipped Cream

Make this cake a day in advance so that it sets thoroughly. Before serving, top with whipped cream and chocolate curls, or simply dust with a mixture of 2 tablespoons confectioners' sugar and 1 teaspoon cocoa powder.

FOR THE CAKE

¾ cup unsalted butter, plus butter for preparing the pan

9 ounces bittersweet or semisweet chocolate, chopped

6 large eggs, separated

⅛ teaspoon salt

⅛ teaspoon cream of tartar

½ cup granulated sugar

⅓ cup firmly packed light brown sugar

1 teaspoon vanilla extract

6 tablespoons all-purpose flour

⅓ cup ground toasted almonds

FOR THE CINNAMON WHIPPED CREAM

¾ cup heavy cream

1 tablespoon confectioners' sugar

1 teaspoon vanilla extract

1 teaspoon ground cinnamon

FOR THE CHOCOLATE CURLS

1 four-ounce bar bittersweet chocolate

Preheat the oven to 350°F. Line the bottom of a 9-inch springform pan with parchment paper, and butter the pan sides.

To make the cake: In a heavy saucepan, melt the ¾ cup butter and the chocolate together over low heat, stirring until smooth. Let cool. In a large bowl, beat the egg whites until foamy, add the salt and cream of tartar, and beat until soft peaks form. Add 3 tablespoons of the granulated sugar, and beat until stiff, glossy peaks form. Set aside.

In a large bowl, beat the egg yolks until thick and lemon colored. Beat in the remaining granulated sugar, the brown sugar, and the vanilla until creamy and smooth. Stir in the chocolate mixture, flour, and almonds. Stir in a third of the egg-white mixture to lighten the batter, and then gently fold in the remaining whites. Pour into the prepared pan, and smooth the top.

Bake for 35 minutes or until set around the sides but still soft in the center. The cake will rise and crack on top. Transfer to a rack and let cool completely in the pan. Wrap the cake with plastic wrap, and store in the refrigerator until serving time. Unmold the cake by putting a serving plate on the cake pan and inverting the plate and pan together. Remove the pan sides and bottom, and carefully peel off the parchment paper.

To make the cinnamon whipped cream: In a cold bowl, whip the cream until soft peaks form. Add the confectioners' sugar, vanilla, and cinnamon, and continue to whip until medium-stiff peaks form. Spread the whipped cream over the top of the cake.

To make the chocolate curls: Hold the chocolate bar with a paper towel and use a vegetable peeler to shave big curls, letting them fall onto a sheet of waxed paper. (You will need only about half of the chocolate; a larger bar is used because it makes forming curls easier.) Slide the curls off the paper onto the whipped cream–topped cake.

MAKES 12 SERVINGS

Keeping Memories

Once the holiday festivities have wound down—but while the memories are still fresh—think about how you might like to preserve your favorite Christmas moments with simple displays, creative storage ideas, and clever ways to reuse holiday cards.

LOVING CONNECTIONS

When Jason and I were newly married, we barely had enough furniture to fill our little apartment. But thanks to our mothers, we had enough ornaments to decorate a Christmas tree—and to start making some holiday memories of our own.

Among the ornaments they gave us were some handcrafted treasures: a cardboard star covered in foil with a picture of Jason, age five, pasted in the center, and a paper Santa face glued to a coffee can lid with "Keely 1979" scrawled on the back. There were special favorites: the gold ornaments Jason had received from his aunt each year, and a little flocked mouse I had always loved finding a perch for. Together they were a loving connection between the families we came from and the one we were starting.

In Jason's box, we found snapshots of him as a boy hanging some of those very ornaments. So we decided to take pictures of each other decorating our first tree. After the holidays, we put our combined ornaments in a bigger box and included an album with both the old and new photos. Now we add a few new ornaments and pictures every year. And we're looking forward to the masterpieces our two young daughters will soon contribute.

Keely Chace

HOLIDAY MEMENTOS

Christmases come and go all too soon, but there are ways to make the magic last. Keepsakes turn memories into something tangible—and holding on to them helps us hold on to the best of the past.

Personalize your holidays by decorating with the heirlooms you treasure: your great-aunt's vintage angel tree topper, ornaments from friends, or the cardboard-and-cotton-ball Santa your son made when he was seven. It's a wonderful way to connect the present with the people and events of Christmases gone by.

The challenge is choosing what to keep and what to let go. Spread out your holiday decorations and group similar items together; then choose the standouts and decide what to pass along or discard. For instance, with kids' artwork, choose favorite pieces, one for each year. Another approach is to pick a single object to represent a significant life stage: a stocking you saved from grade school, a cross-stitched ornament you made in college, and the First Christmas Together ball you got for your wedding.

Creating themed collections is another way to organize your treasures. Your children's hospital bracelets, baby shoes, and silver rattles make sweet decorations for a small tree. Your grandmother's collection of mercury-glass ornaments, now supplemented by ones from your mother and those you've collected yourself, reminds you of the bond of love that unites the women in your family.

Could your kids really have been that small?
Mementos like photos with Santa transport
you back to the joys of Christmases past.

HOLIDAY 2006

A scrapbook is a great way to hold on to holiday joy. Jot down some favorite memories, and tuck in photos, letters to Santa, and other keepsakes.

Think beyond photographs when you're creating a scrapbook. Pull together an assortment of memorabilia to remind you of the people and events that made your holiday special. Get the entire family involved by letting everyone create his or her own personal pages.

• Choose a book that can have pages added after each Christmas, or compile a new scrapbook each year. Buy one with pockets (or add your own) to hold items like gift lists and party invitations.

• A great way to remember presents—and the people who gave them—is to make a "wreath" from that year's gift tags (left).

• Pieces of gift wrap, cutouts from Christmas cards, and even pressed holiday flowers can be used to decorate your book. Or you might adorn the cover with bows made out of ribbon saved from the gifts you received that year (right).

• When you've finished your scrapbook, tuck the book away until next Christmas. When the holiday season rolls around again, plan a special night for your family to pull out the scrapbook, relive memories, and gear up for the season ahead.

Use the Christmas cards you send and receive each year to create mementos that double as tree decorations.

Sometimes you want to save just part of a card you received—the message, a photo, some artwork. Making a card garland is an easy way to do this. It's also fun to fashion three-dimensional ornaments out of the cards you send each year.

● To make the ornament, cut four same-sized circles from a card (depending on the design, you might use more than one card). On the blank sides of three of the circles, draw an equilateral triangle with its corners touching the circle's edge. Fold the paper up along the sides of each triangle. Glue folded edges of the three circles together to form a pyramid. Write the year on the unfolded circle, and glue it to the base. Using a long needle, thread ribbon through the center, attaching a jingle bell at the bottom and forming a loop on top.

● To make the garland, cut out circles from cards, focusing on favorite holiday images, messages, and smiling faces. Cut two slits near opposing edges of each circle, and slide a shimmering ribbon through the slits to string the cards together.

Ornament Care

Before packing ornaments away, wipe each one clean with a damp rag and air dry. Make any needed repairs, such as touching up chips or regluing parts.

Take a photo of ornaments before packing them in a box, and tape it to the outside, so that it's easy to find what you're looking for next year.

If an ornament has several pieces, pack them together to make it easier to assemble the next year.

Because extreme cold or heat can damage ornaments, store them in a temperature-controlled space.

Heirloom ornaments are special because they remind us of the people and places of our past.

Sharing Heirlooms (above left) When your kids start having homes and Christmas trees of their own, pass on some treasured ornaments to remind them of the holidays you've shared as a family.

Sweet Stitches (left) Ornaments such as these beaded songbirds can be fashioned from fabric that has special meaning. For example, consider creating ornaments from a baby blanket or a favorite but ragged hand-knit sweater.

Christmas Cookies (right) Everyday items such as your mother's hand-me-down cookie cutters can be heirlooms, too. Display cookie cutters at Christmas by turning them into ornaments. Attach backings made from cards or gift wrap. Glue ribbon around the edges, and knot it on top.

Collections are meant to be enjoyed. So bring them out of the trunk or cupboard, dust them off, and display them prominently in unexpected places throughout your home.

Snowy Souvenirs (left) Ceramic Santas (and the odd penguin) bring North Pole freshness to a mudroom windowsill. To keep a piece from falling, secure it with tape, or try a museum trick and use adhesive wax or putty (sold at hardware stores and online). Before using any adhesive, make sure it won't damage a collectible or its display surface.

Special Collection (above) Silver napkin rings can be used on the dinner table, but they also make a striking display when collected in a bowl.

Tree Time (right) A forest of tiny trees sprouts from a table. A common element, the pearlescent balls tucked into the tree branches, visually connects the collection pieces on display.

Make a family Christmas time capsule. Gather and pack away items that capture the sights, smells, and sounds of this holiday season to enjoy in the years ahead.

Your Christmas time capsule doesn't have to be large or fancy. Choose a clear box about the size of a DVD storage box so that you can store it easily and see the contents at a glance.

● Add the year's bundle of holiday cards, gift lists, letters to Santa, party invitations, and perhaps a few special ornaments, such as the ones inscribed with the wishes of family and friends (see page 75). You might also want to include copies of photos and videotapes as backups for your originals. Label the box with large letters to make it easy to find.

● Stash your time capsule in a safe place, and decide when you will open it. Some families choose to open the capsule five or ten years from its inception date. Others pull out the time capsules every year to watch old videos and glean inspiration from past Christmas lists.

● As you build up your collection of capsules, store them together so that they're easy to find when you feel like creating a little holiday spirit.

INDEX

ACKNOWLEDGMENTS

All photography by Ellen Silverman except for the following:

Hallmark Cards, Inc., pages 8, 10, 12, 19, 21 (upper right), 28–29, 31–33, 43 (top), 46, 70, 104, 106, 140, 142, 150, 160.

Justin Bernhaut, pages 35, 39 (left), 56, 65 (right), 109, 135, 145–147, 151.

Emma Boys, page 123.

Weldon Owen wishes to thank everyone at Hallmark who contributed ideas, support, and enthusiasm for this book, especially Peg Anderson-Lee, Lisa Beel, Angela Ensminger, Mary Gentry, Todd Hafer, Jeff Morgan, Tracey Petrie, Brad Rinehart, Stacy Schaffer, Becky Smith, Kevin Swanson, and Megan Walsh.

We gratefully acknowledge editorial assistance from Donita Boles, Sophie Giles, Lucie Parker, and Hannah Rahill, and design assistance from Gaye Allen, Britt Staebler, Renée Myers, Anna Migirova, and Lisa Milestone. We would like to thank the following for contributing to the production of this book:

Photography Assistants: Michael Bennett, Tom Hood. Stylist's Assistants: Daniele Maxwell, Alan Snyder. Food Stylists: Kevin Crafts, Shelly Kaldunski, Jen Straus. Food Stylists' Assistants: Alexa Hyman, Max La Rivière-Hedrick. Caterers: William Cooper, Kass Kapsiak. Homeowners: Andy and Kerry Bogardus, William and Kelly Cooper, Carol and John Knorpp, Greg and Aimee Price, Susan and John Rosenberg. Models: Natalie Bogardus; Noel Borg and Betsy Fabro-Borg; Emma Conneely; Ann Marie Cooper; Tracey, Alex, and Max Diaz; Sophie Giles; Shayla Lemos; Claire and Markham Johnson; Amy Marr; Philip Milestone; Julia Nelson; Jim Nickovich; Emma Claire and Olivia Price with Lulu and Lilly; Marsha, Charlie, and Tommy Quanstrom; Britt Staebler.

Ellen Silverman would like to thank Josh and Luca for continuous love, patience, and support, and for gracefully enduring my absences while I worked on this project; Emma, Amy, Lauren, and Michael for your keen eyes, long hours, and quick wit, without which we would not have created such a beautiful book.

Lauren Hunter wishes to thank my family for creating and sharing holidays that inspire my work; the team at Weldon Owen; Ellen for her patience and skill in photographing the images; the staffs at Chelsea Antiques, Copper Home and Garden, I Leoni, Sienna Antiques, and Summer Cottage Antiques—all in Petaluma, California—who provided many of the unique accessories included here.

If you have enjoyed this book, Hallmark would love to hear from you.

Please send comments to:
Book Feedback
2501 McGee, Mail Drop 215
Kansas City, MO 64141-6580

or e-mail us at:
booknotes@hallmark.com
www.hallmark.com

May your home be filled with
many wonderful holiday moments.